South African Stories

South African Stories

True Stories of Faith, Hardship
and Deliverance
from the Hearts and Pens
of Black South Africans

Dan Cole
Editor

North Wind Publishing
Camden, Maine

North Wind Publishing
P.O. Box 192
Rockport, ME 04856
www.northwindpublishing.com

10 9 8 7 6 5 4 3 2 1

ISBN 0-9720620-1-7

Library of Congress Control Number 2003101006

Edited by Pamela Benner

Contents

Introduction

The writings on the following pages are from the hearts and pens of black South Africans. By themselves they reflect how God has made a significant impact on their lives and are warm reminders of how God reaches across our planet to touch the lives of people everywhere.

Yet the material they have written takes on deeper meaning when placed in the context of their culture, their recent history and, in some cases, their language expressions. An understanding of the legacy of apartheid, the place of women in society and what it is like to be abused makes these reflections even more powerful.

To know what it is like to be raised with racial hatred makes Luvuyo Ntombana's story of color convicting. To know that Sipho Khanyile is a Zulu pastor whose daughter was gang raped, the culprits caught, brought to trial and then released by the magistrate, makes his poem "The Other Side" heart wrenching.

I hope you will be blessed by these writing as I was blessed by knowing each of the authors.

—Dan Cole

Publishers Note: Minimal editing was done to preserve the voice, character and culture of the writers. The editors chose to clarify only when meaning was in doubt.

South African Stories

▼

A Demon of Fire

David Moloi

O ne family in Dlamini had problems with a demon of fire. There was a young man in that family by the name of Roxy [not his real name]. Roxy had money to spend on buying expensive clothes. It was then he said that some jealous people bewitched him by sending fire to consume all the expensive clothes he had. The demon of fire would come down through the ceiling and destroy everything in that room belonging to Roxy. The ceiling would remain intact, as well as the paint on the wall would not get burned up.

Many people were requested to come and drive out the evil spirit, but all failed. Witch doctors were also consulted. They also failed to drive out the evil spirit. The family had already lost all hope when one of the relatives requested us to come and help them.

We were a group of about eight Christians. We agreed to observe a one-day fasting and prayer. That particular evening we went to Roxy's home and spent a short time of presenting Jesus to the entire family. We realized that it would not do them any good for us to cast out the devil if they still belonged to him. They all responded to the altar call, and we prayed with them a sinner's prayer.

The business of driving out the demon began. We moved from one room to another, destroying the devil in the name of Jesus. We even went to an extent of opening windows and commanded the demons to go out in the name of Jesus. When

we got into Roxy's room, we felt the heavy presence of evil spirits. The hair on our arms moved. Praise and glory to God that we all stayed focused in Christ. Had it not been the enveloping presence of God in our lives, we all would have ran away without saying a word to each other. Every one of us was calling the name of Jesus Christ as we opened the windows for the devil to go out. We again assembled in the living room to give thanks to God.

The family then brought a big pot which they got from one of the Witch doctors. It contained a "muti" (a spirit). We destroyed that "muti" in the name of Jesus. As we gathered there in the living room, thanking and praising god, we heard a big bang on the door, and that was the last of the demon of fire. It was destroyed by the Almighty God who is "A consuming fire," Hebrews 12:29.

All praise and glory be given to God. To this day, Roxy's family has never experienced any harassment from or by a demon of fire. Glory to God that there is not, and never has been, any devil that could stand against the name of Jesus Christ. He is the same yesterday, today and forever, Amen.

A Victim

Sipho Khanyile

Why am I victimized in this manner?
Is it my beauty that I suffer for?
Perhaps it is for my feminine appearance?
How long will I be humiliated and abused in this way?
Why I am turned to be a victim of the circumstances?
Come on people answer me how long?

Why are people so ungracious and cunning?
Where is your humanity, compassionate spirit?
When will you change your attitude and behavior?
When will your joy over our shame cease?
Your status as men has been dragged into the mud.
Here is no gentleness in the gentleman.

Our tears and laments have been shed in the hills and forest
Even in our own homes we weep aloud
Tell us! How loud should we cry so that you will hear our cry?
Our place as a woman is no longer something to be proud of
We have been turned into rabbits among dogs or pigeon
among cats.
Where are the prudent men of this country?

Are there no men of justice in our country,
no upright men?
Why are you insensitive in our pain and agony?
For how long will you be silent about our predicament?
We are molested and slain in front of statesmen
and public protectors
Are you afraid of these cannibals and barbarians?
You have authority and power vested upon you.
May we remind you that we still are a
majority in this country

Will you please answer the following questions?
Have your statistics ready.
How many innocent women have been abused
raped and killed?
How many innocent children were abused
sodomized and killed?
How many old people, our ancestors, are abused
raped and killed?
How many fathers and husbands were condemned
for what they have not done?
How long South Africa you will turn a blind eye
and deaf ear to our cries?

Deliverance

Thandeka

There's a time in my life I questioned God's existence. Part of me believed there is God somewhere, but I had a problem with His manner of love. My small mind couldn't understand why other people are sad while others are happy, others poor while others are rich. If He is a kind God as people say, why can't He make all people happy and rich? If He is Love, why can't I feel His love, why can't He give me the love I long for more than anything else?

I was a young and inexperienced girl who has been through tough times. I was carrying a load, suffering from the consequences of abuse, abandonment and lack of supportive family. My mother was working in Gauteng, thousands of kilometers away from Sterkstroom, where I grew up. I was staying with my grandma's sister. My father abandoned me when I was five. My aunt took me and promised to take care of me. I was three years then. I can't remember what she looked like. All I know is that she ruined my childhood. She physically abused me. I was told that the last time she beat me I had to be taken to hospital. I was dying. My whole body and head were swollen. She then disappeared and was never seen again. My oldest sister kept on telling my grandma, but she never believed her because she was also young. I swam on the sea of my blood with no one to rescue me.

I cannot recall what it was like in those moments but

believe me, every time I close my eyes I could see a little girl with bleeding wounds, with tears on her little face. I could see the terror, the confusion, the pain on her eyes. I could see her, begging for mercy in front of a monstrous woman. I could see her groaning in pains and I know who she is—that little girl is me, Thandeka.

After I recovered I was taken to my grandma's house. Nobody understood or cared about me. My world was turned upside down. I was an unhappy little girl, I was lonely, withdrawn and terrified. I was longing for love. I needed someone to love me and to hold me close and tell me that I am safe. But, there was no one. I was carrying a load, a suitcase full of sorrows, terror, pain and misery.

I carried my heavy load up to my teen years. I went to High School and did very well in my studies. All my teachers admired me. I was a hard worker and everyone thought I was a happy girl. I was not, I was empty inside, I was devastated. It was as if the whole world was on my shoulders.

In 1994 I was doing Grade 9 and was 16. One Friday afternoon, a guy came to me and invited me to attend a S.C.M. service (Student Christian Movement). They were holding services every Friday afternoon after school. I never liked going to church. "What's the use of going to church, nobody loves me and God himself doesn't love me," I thought. I promised to come although I knew that was the last thing I wanted to do. Something urged me to go there and I tried so hard to resist. I ended up going. It was a cold and rainy day, the 27th May 1994. There were only a few students who attended that day. The guy who invited me was preaching. He was talking about Jesus, the Bread of Life. I can't really recall everything he was saying but after the sermon I was convinced that I need Jesus. I lifted my hand with those who needed to accept Jesus as Lord and Savior. I was not really sure of what I was doing. It was like I'm dreaming. All I know is that my heart was changed. I was transformed, I was healed, and I was forgiven. I was comforted but most of all I was LOVED. Jesus was now my friend and every thing to me. He calmed my fears. He soothed my sorrows. I was set free. My burden was taken away. I will never forget the joy that filled my heart since that day. Jesus was there for me all those times. He felt those pains. He cried those tears. He was with me in that situation. He is that someone I was looking for. I was delivered.

I never cease to thank God for the guy who used to pull me from my dark world and put me into His light. His name was Luvuyo Ntombana. He is now a Pastor. He is a father to me, and a brother and a good friend.

Train Ministry

David Moloi

I t all began with a question that was too heavy for me. I could not bear it. "Look at all these people in this coach." I looked at them, "Where do you think they will go when they die?" I believed that God was challenging me to be His ambassador.

I responded positively to the challenge and started preaching the Gospel. I was scared when I started, but the Lord helped me. There were many objections from the commuters, some of which were very scary. I remember one particular morning when I got into a particular coach, which was full of smoke from "dagga" [marijuana], which the guys smoked. I must confess that I had to make a special prayer before I went to preach in that coach. Many preachers would not dare to preach there. As I started to preach, one guy shouted at me never ever to preach in that coach. He had a very bad scar on his face. That made him look like he was possessed or in that state of anger. I felt led to ignore him. When I finished preaching I climbed off, and that very guy warned me never to set my foot in that coach again.

I went back to God and prayed that He will protect and strengthen me as I intended to go back into that coach to preach the Gospel. The following morning I went to preach in that coach again. To my surprise, Mr. Scar was not there, and

the Lord softened the hearts of those there to listen. I preached for four days in that coach and never saw Mr. Scar. Even though there was no positive commitment, the commuters in that coach were happy to listen to the preaching of the Word. God dealt with that situation in such a way that I felt encouraged to go on because He was working within me.

One day as I was preaching, in came about eight policemen who were patrolling. One of them requested me to produce a ticket, which I gave to him while preaching. They then commanded me never to preach as I was disturbing the peace in that coach. Those policemen decided not to proceed into another coach as if they wanted to see if I would continue to preach or not. I tried to keep quiet, but I could not. The Word of God was burning in my heart. I just could not bear it. Then I heard God speaking to me saying: "Are you going to obey man who tells you not to preach, or God who has sent you to preach?" All eyes were glued on me, including the police. I found myself continuing where I left off before the police came. I preached on.

One lady advised me not to continue preaching. I told her, "I am prepared to be arrested for preaching God's Word." Praise God that those policemen also heard the Word of God preached to them and God never allowed them to touch me.

Then one morning after preaching from Mlamlankunzi station Langloagle, the sliding doors of the train would not open for us to climb off. I ran to the next door, and it also would not open. I went for the nearest window to jump out. As soon as I put my body forward to jump out, I fell back into the train. By that time the train was moving. I tried to jump for the second time, and the same thing happened. I cannot explain how that happened, but it was a nice feeling. It was like a gentle breeze kept pushing me back inside the coach. I decided to give up, and climbed off at the next station, Mayfair, where I got a train to Randfontein.

When we got to Langloagle, I found that many people who jumped out of the other train's window were arrested. Had God not intervened by pushing me back into the coach, I would have been arrested as well. Think of a pastor in handcuffs! God is a good God. When He sends you, He provides. He provided protection for me so that I did not get into trouble by jumping through the train's window.

God revealed Himself to me as the Great God who works with me in many ways during my train ministry. It gives me such joy and thanksgiving to God as I meet my children in the Lord in many areas of Gauteng. Thank God that my labor in the Lord was not in vain. May the good Lord take all the glory for the work that He accomplished with me in the train ministry.

Baby's Rights

Sipho Khanyile

I am a Baby! A child! Who is a human being
Please don't take an advantage of my Ignorance
and Innocence
The fact is that every Baby has the right to exist
I also have the right to cry and sing songs in my
own language
I have the right to spoon feed and breast feed of my
mother's milk
I have the right to own clean napkins [diapers], warm
clothes and bed
Therefore do not deprive me of my rights I know them.

If I cry or sometimes become restless don't be offended
This is my only way of conveying my message to you
Instead, offer relief from the wet napkin and attend to
my hunger
Please don't get offended. Instead study my habits
Then you will be my friend and love will be our
language together
Life will be a joyful exercise if my rights are respected
Please respect my rights and never take advantage of me.

The truth is that I never ever chose to be a baby
Nor to be your child or to own your surname
Once I am conceived in my mother's womb I then have
the right to live
No one has the right to take my life by any means
I have great value to God and to many others in the World
Please take me to people who have love for those like me.

I have the right of good caring parents and neat home
My right is to be raised well and not to be confused
I have the right to be loved and to be comfortable
in all respects
It is my right to be educated and be clothed respectfully
It is my right to be mothered and to be well looked after
I have the right to be told about God and His Love
Please do not hide the facts of life to me, but teach me.

Remember you were the only one who had a choice
of having me
Since I now exist, grant me a normal life
To be your Baby does not mean that I can be handled
in just any way
Please give me the love that I deserve not the love
that is full of lust
Just listen careful to what I am to say to you now
I possess the right of living whether I am handicapped
or normally born
Once I am conceived I am God's creation.

Zulu Sunday school children.

Neighborhood children in the township of Mandeni.

Zulu boy in traditional dress of animal skins.

Children of Venda (northern South Africa).

Zulu children singing of the Joy of the Lord.

Hijackers

David Moloi

It was in the late nineteen eighties when I bought a Super 10 mini bus from my boss. I had only made three monthly payments of R500-00 per month when I fell into the hands of three hijackers. The sun had just gone down when I arrived from work. I parked the mini bus on the driveway, rushed into our main bedroom where my wife was sick with flu. I had just greeted her, and just before I could find out from her as to how she was feeling, there was a knock on the bedroom door. When I opened the door, it was my son, who then told me that some men wanted to see me.

I went out through the back door and met three guys who told me that they were selling spare parts for a Super Ten mini bus. Well, it was and still is my policy never to buy spare parts sold from door to door. Hence, I told those guys that I did not have any need for spare parts, as my mini bus was okay. Before I could do or say anything, one of the guys pulled out a gun and threatened to shoot me if I did not comply. A cold shrill ran through my body. I became fearful. Another guy pulled out a knife, while the third one had a beer bottle in his hand. I was ordered to go into the mini bus and show them how to start it. At that time, the guy with a gun ran into the house and forced my mother-in-law, my son and daughter into the main bedroom. He threatened to shoot them if they came out. He then came out and joined the other two with me in the mini bus. I showed them how to get the mini bus started and off they went with me.

I realized that death was staring me in the face. Silently, I called upon the Lord to save me. Immediately all fear disappeared. The Holy Spirit took over. He gave me scriptures and enabled me to believe God to fulfill them. Some of these scripture verses are Isaiah 54:17 "No weapon forged against you will prevail." Psalm 23:1,4 "The Lord is my Shepherd, I shall lack nothing. Even though I walk through the valley of the shadow of death, I will fear no evil, for you are with me." The more these verses ran through my mind, the more I relaxed. There were moments when they asked me some questions and I never heard them because I was reciting the Word.

I looked at the guy with a gun, and he told me never to look at him and hit me with a fist. He hit me with his full force, and guess what? It was as though he hit me with a small piece of sponge. The guy with a gun was at that stage, fuming with anger. He then ordered the other one with a knife to stab me to death. He could not because the hand that held a knife could not hold the knife firmly. He himself had already failed to pull the trigger. The same guy with a gun, who seemed to be their boss, instructed the guy with a knife to strangle me with my tie. He obeyed, but his hands had no strength to pull the tie.

The driver brought the mini bus to a stand still in a dark secluded spot. I want to give all the glory to God because all along I was at peace with myself. No human being can or could have experienced the calmness the way I did unless God was in control over that situation. I was then ordered to strip naked. They threw me out of the bus and drove off. Within seconds, the Lord provided an ambulance, which seemed to have been ready to pick me up and take me back to my family at home. The ambulance attendants gave me a blanket to put on to cover my nakedness.

That is how the Lord saved me from the hands of the hijackers. All glory to God.

God's Measure

Sipho Khanyile

No one can measure God's wisdom
No one I say
Even His angels cannot
No one can measure His wisdom.

No one can measure God's love
No one yes no one can
Even the scientists cannot
No one can no matter what.

No man can know His secrets
No man, not even one
Even those who are His
No one can, truly none.

No man can reason with God
Only the Christ can
For Christ, you are God
Yes, you are part of the Holy One.

Never Quit

James Setshogelo

Life has its ups and downs
Every year many men leave their families
The walking out of men in their homes
Brings about sadness and loss
Love lost and pain are alike
Devastation becomes a family friend.

Good men don't leave
No matter what happens
Good men will stick around
How hard it may seem
Good fathers will be there.

When a father quits his family
Children often become very lonely, angry and wild.
All along I was looking
For a father he was gone
Just like a snow
When the sun melts it away.

Men who leave their families
Have their pathetic reason
But most are not prepared to confess
Maybe if they did confess
They could help the family to understand them better.

But one thing is for sure
Winners never quit and quitters never win!
Good men never quit.

It has been in fashion now
It differs from one father to the other
The question may be
Why they leave their families
To some, they are running from responsibility
To some, they have found a better place
To some, beautiful women
To some, a better way to destroy themselves
Not only themselves, but they destroy their families.

Hear my words you men out there
Never quit your family
Never think that there is life without problems
Good fathers build their homes
But good men build their families.

Saved

William Mokgatle

How God found my friend is a miracle as he was the most difficult person to be tackled, especially when you share the Good News with him. This friend of mine was fully committed to the life of using *mutis,* trusted *inyangas* and *angomas* [all traditional healers and witch doctors]. He was possessed and believed what he was told his ancestors said. The life style he lived was sinful. He used to despise us a lot that we believe in a person we have never seen before. He called us stupid.

Once on a bright sunny day I asked him to follow me to an open-air fellowship. He did not refuse. The preaching was relevant to his lifestyle and it challenged him. God touched him when all what he used to do was revealed openly. He said to me, "It is like they are playing my biographical life before everyone." Immediately he started crying as the message was exposing him. At the conclusion when the alter call came, he rushed in front to receive and accept Christ as his savior. From that moment and time he never looked back. He is a powerful Christian fully devoted to the word and mission in action.

Suicide

William Mokgatle

I used to have depression attacks when I was all by myself. I would go to people, share with them my problems and come back knowing that they said nothing to help my problem. This used to haunt me a lot as I was not happy at home about how things were run. I could not resolve the problems. I was ignored when I try to voice out my dilemma. The whole thing used to boil me up. I could find no solution. It all fell on deaf ears.

Until a little voice said to me go to Youth Alive Center. This is the place where your problems will be answered. Indeed God saved me as the sermon was directly related to my situation.

A Christian brother who committed suicide was the center of the preaching. God directly challenged me to have peace with him, peace with myself, peace with other people. God healed me completely and lifted me up to my senses.

It Is Not Yet Uhuru

(a day that celebrates liberation)

William Mokgatle

It is not yet uhuru
For there is plenty of work
In your vineyard Lord.
The laborers are few.

It is not yet uhuru
For many are called
Into your house Lord.
But, few are eager to work.

It is not yet uhuru
Though many are called
Few are chosen
To be partners with you.

It is not yet uhuru
You never rested
You worked around the clock
You never ceased in your work.

It is not yet uhuru
Your desire is that we preach
Your gospel to others
So that together we may reach the world.

It is not yet uhuru
Till your truth has reached every man
Until our ministries together are completed
Then it will be **uhuru** in heaven.

Salvation for the Poor?

William Mokgatle

If salvation was only for the poor
It would not have reached me
It would have passed over me
It would not have found its place among my coins.

If salvation was only for the hungry
It would not have reached me
It would slip over me
It would have not found its place at my table.

If salvation was only for the unwanted
It would not have caught me
It would have forgotten me
It would not have found its place in my family.

If salvation was only for the lonely
It would not have settled in me
It would have given up on me
It would not have found its place among my friends.

If salvation was only for the wicked
It would not have encompassed me
It would not have sought me
It would not have found me while I prayed.

If salvation was only for the unfortunate
It would not have engulfed me
It would not have hold on my life
But, praise God, salvation is for everyone.

Jealousy Kills

James Setshogelo

The Bible lays down a great commandment
It is all about love
We are to love our neighbors
For all they have become
For who they are
Oh Jealousy! Oh Jealousy!

Lack of confidence
Lack of love, and belonging
Look at what it has brought
People do not love their neighbors
Some neighbors are sick
Some are rich
Some are poor
But these do not matter
Jealousy has brought death into the community.

Jealousy kills the soul inside each of us
When you are never satisfied
With all you have.
Churches have been destroyed
Families have been destroyed
Relationship has been destroyed
Why, why must this continue to happen?

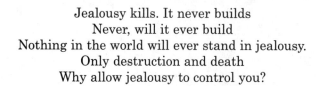

Jealousy kills. It never builds
Never, will it ever build
Nothing in the world will ever stand in jealousy.
Only destruction and death
Why allow jealousy to control you?

Jesus My Friend

James Setshogelo

Just when I need you
It seems you are there
What a help and encouragement you are Jesus
Just knowing that you care
When I'm alone
It's so nice to have a friend like you Jesus
You are special
Jesus you are special.

So loving
So true
So kind
Oh Jesus my special friend

O, Lord, I want to say to you
Our friendship is golden and pure
Costly and real
Our friendship is like precious china
Costly and rare
If broken it cannot hardly be mended.

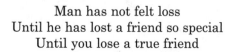

Man has not felt loss
Until he has lost a friend so special
Until you lose a true friend

The rain may fall
The wind may blow
But my love for Jesus
Will never fade or die.

Color

Luvuyo Ntombana

I grew up in Northern Cape region in a small town called Hanover. This small town is divided into three communities. There is one community each, for white, colored and black people. This is one of the places where black people were badly treated by white people. I remember going to a shop where I would find two doors to the shop. One is for blacks the other for white people. This kind of life made me think that we were created to be inferior to white people.

I was born in the 1970s during the time of political uprisings in South Africa. This did not affect me much because I was still young. I remember 1985. I was ten years old by then. At home I was staying with my cousins. I am told that my father passed away in the gold mine, I never saw him. My mother was working as a domestic worker in Johannesburg. It was the time when many black people were tortured and killed. My cousin was very active in politics.

One evening, it was around 12 o'clock when the police came to look for him. There were several tall and strong Afrikaans [white] people. There were two of us in the house, I was 10 years and my younger cousin was 7 years old. They knocked for a long time and I did not open the door. They then decided to break the window and come in. They said, *"ey kaffir,"* insulting words to the Xhosas [tribe]. They asked us where our cousin was. I said that I didn't know.

"When did you last see him?"

I said, "last night he was here with us and I don't know where he is now."

They beat both of us and in my face I still have a scar that reminds me of that day. Then they took us inside the hepo [armored vehicle]. They promised to beat me until I told them the truth. While they were taking us to the hepo my cousin appeared. I don't know where he was coming from. Growing up with such experiences made me hate white people.

Between 1984 and 1987 a lot of black people were killed in this small town. This violence caused my mother to decide to move us to a place called Ciskeio, which was Xhosa homeland. Things became better for me here. I stayed in a rural area in a village where there were no white or colored people.

Even when I accepted the Lord in my life, I still hated white people. I remember in 1995 I went to visit my sister in Cape Town. She works as a domestic worker in Muzenberg. I was allowed to stay with her in her room at the backyard of the Master's house. One of the rules she gave me was to smile and laugh whenever I talk to her employers (Madam & Master). I did not like this, but I promised to do so because I wanted to stay with her. I could not pretend, I hated these white people. As a result, my sister gave me train fare and sent me home before finishing even one week.

In 1996 I was doing my first year at the college. While I was studying I was also working a part-time job at the Baptist Convention office in Johannesburg. I remember that visitors and volunteers from overseas used to come and visit the office. Most of them were white. They were very nice people but I did not like them.

I was the victim here because I was also staying in the same community. Whenever these visitors wanted to take a walk or go somewhere, others would say, "Ask Luvuyo." Some of these visitors realized that I was running away from them. What is funny is, this made them more curious to know the reason why I was avoiding them.

In the same year two white missionaries came from the U.S.A. It was a man and his wife. One of the college students named Andile got used to these missionaries. I asked him how they were. He said the wife is a nice person but he is not sure about the man. The problem started when I had to do some work with the man missionary. We had to run errands together and I also had to report to him whenever I needed some help concerning my job. Because I was running away from him, this caused some problems in my work. Before the end of the month I got used to both of them. I did not know how to call them, everybody was calling them Dan and Sandy, because of their age I called them Papa and Mama. As I got used to them they became my father and mother. Our friendship made me realize that there is nothing wrong with the color of the skin of people. Honestly speaking, this idea took some time to form in my head. At first it was difficult to understand how could they love me. I am such a poor black young man. Then I realized that they were not pretending but our friendship was genuine. We then planted a Church in Johannesburg. This work gave us an opportunity to know each other better.

Even though I realized that there is nothing wrong with the color of someone's skin, I sometimes had some disagreements with Papa Dan. I would always think it is because I'm black and he is white. This took a long time for me to understand that this had nothing to do with color. I realized that he was protective and also he was just like any other old man in my community. My relationship with them played a very important role in my life. I felt that the Lord was really at work in my life. This changed the way I treated people. Even now when I see a person, I don't think of the color of their skin but I see a brother or a sister. I have realized that in each and every human being there is more than just a color. We are all created in God's image. There were times I even spoke in Xhosa (my home language) with Papa Dan and Mama Sandy, forgetting that they are white and could only speak English. Now what comes first to me is the person before I ever see color. I thank God for delivering me from this disease of color.

Luvuyo Ntombana.

The Rev. Sipho Khanyile.

South African women sing at a regional meeting.

Self-Acceptance

James Setshogelo

Lord Jesus I never had a smooth life
From childhood to now nearing five decades
Lord you know why
Why it had to be so.

Lord Jesus I never had a happy life
From before I knew you even after knowing you
Lord you know why
Why it had to be so.

Lord I never had Jesus
From the cradle until you found me
Lord you know why
Why it had to be so.

Lord Jesus instill in me strength
From time to time to hold me fast
Lord, you too never had an easy life.
You were born in a stable and died on a cross.

Jesus teach me self-acceptance
Teach me to know that you have been where I am
You are Lord of all circumstances
You Lord, know why I am as I am.

Lord Jesus pour your spirit upon me.
Empower me to preach thy gospel without regard of myself.
Lord of all seasons nothing escapes you,
Not even whom you have made me to be.

Makie

Thandeka

I came to know Makie in 1998. I loved her smile. I enjoyed listening to her each time we had discussions. She knew the Word of God. She loved the Lord with all her heart and she was active in the church. I admired her. I always wanted to talk to her but I was shy. She was a student in Vaal Triangle Technikon, doing her first year. I was so drawn to her and in time we started talking. She was so wise, so intelligent. We became good friends.

We had so much in common. We both knew how it feels to sail on the sea of sufferings and pains. Her mother was not working for money but for a plate of food and a little room to sleep. At home she had one brother and two sisters, they were younger than her. She stayed and looked after them while she was still at High School. After she passed Matric she had to leave them alone to go to Technikon. That was the hardest thing to do, but she did it. She managed to get financial help for registration. She was later dumped and had to find her own way of paying all the fees. There was no source of income in the family. God fed all of them. He's the one who determined their next meal. She was suffering. Where she was staying she had to pay rent and buy food. I always thought I suffered more than anyone else, but after listening to her stories, I knew I was better off.

One day I invited her to visit me. I couldn't believe it when she told me that she hadn't eaten for two days. I was so thankful that God used me to feed His starving child. We sat in my room and started pouring our sorrows onto each other. She was always talking about the children she left at home. She knew they were starving to death and there was nothing she could do. She was distressed. She told me about a dream she once had that really touched me. I am not a person who believes much in dreams but when she was telling me about hers, I couldn't stop my tears from running down. I will let her tell it to you herself.

I dreamed I was in the church. Someone came and forced me to give up my seat for this girl. All who came were against me. They were all laughing at me. I went out crying. There was a strong wind blowing outside. I wanted to go home but I was afraid because the rain was coming. The dark and thick clouds started to form in the sky. There was no one to take me home so I decided to run as fast as I could. It became darker and darker. I was so terrified. The heavy rain came and thunders started to roar. I kept on running. I was alone and it was now even darker. The only thing that lit my way was the flashing of lightning. I saw someone coming toward me. It was one brother from the church where I attended at home. He was trustworthy and a devoted man of god. He was worried about me. We walked together, stumbling and falling. Suddenly there was a big river before us. To get home I had to cross this river.

The brother looked at me and said, "Makie, I'm sorry but this is where my journey ends."

I saw him turning his back on me. I was alone once more. I stood there crying. There was nothing I could do so I jumped into that huge and overflowing river and that was the end of my dream.

Some people might think this is a Disneyland story, but there is a lot of reality in it. Friends and lovers can go miles with you, they can stand with you through the storms, through the darkest nights and through it all, but there is always a quitting point. There is always a time when you are forced to walk the dark valleys of death alone. There's a time when you have to sail on the river of your own sorrows alone. Everything that happened in her life kept reminding her of her dream. After she finished telling me about her dream, there was quietness and the tears started to roll down our faces. She looked at me and said, "Thandeka, when will I get through it, please tell me, when? For how long must I suffer?" She asked those questions and I knew they were coming from deep inside a torn and crushed heart. "I don't know when Makie, I really don't know, but you'll get through it." That was all I could say.

She was forced to quit school. Her results were blocked because she had no money. She was so desperate and vulnerable and that made her believe all the promises that were made to her. She faced disappointments from the Christians who promised to help her and later dumped her. They raised her hopes and made her believe that they were trustworthy. She was crushed in spirit but she never gave up. She kept on trusting God in that situation.

Today I am very proud to tell you that she did get through. She is now working for a certain Christian family with a Public phone business. Her mother is no longer working to get a plate of food. God shone His light on her. When she was walking through the dark valleys of death, God was with her. When she was passing through that dark river, God was there with her. God held her by His right hand and was saying, "Do not fear, I'm with you." She was not alone. One day we'll sit to talk again but this time we'll be pouring out our joys to each other. We'll be telling of the goodness of God. We will continue to shed tears. But, they will be tears of joy.

Marriage

Luvuyo Ntombana

In the olden days, it was accepted that parents had to choose for their children who to marry. It is surprising to hear that this is still happening in some villages in Ciskeio. One of the ladies at the university told me her experience of this custom. This happened in 1998, by then she was 19 years old and doing her matric [tests]. Her parents approached her and told her that she should stop going to school because she is a grown up woman now. At least she can write a letter and it can come back.

At the same time her brothers were still at school and one of them in the university. When she was told of this she had a feeling that something is coming. In the same month she noticed that there were people who came to her home that she did not know. You can easily identify when people are coming for serious business. The way they would wear big coats and hats, and you also see that it will be old men that are trusted by their families. She did not know what was really happening and they were also withholding this from her. All this she was told by her younger brother. As he was telling her, he was already rejoicing that his sister was going to get married. This news was bad news to this young lady who wanted to further her studies. In the same week she was called by her parents, they told her that someone from a respected family wants to marry her. They never asked her to respond to that. She did not like this arrangement but there was nothing she could do. She told herself that she must go to this family and obey this custom. Because this was some time away, she did not bother to think about it. It was the day she saw eight cows coming to the yard, then she realized that this is true.

The following month she was taken to her new home. In this home she was among four young men. It was not too bad to get married to them. She told herself she will get used to it. She was wrong. She was introduced to an old man. He was more than forty years old and looked as old as her father. She immediately got nervous and fell down. They were not caring towards her, what they did was just to help her stand on her feet and gave her water to drink. This lady says what made her collapse is to realize that her parents did not love her. They are only concerned about money and satisfying their friends.

This was her first day here in the strange home. As she was working this old man kept on saying my wife is so beautiful. The night is coming. Tonight will be the night. He seemed to rejoice that he was going to bed with her. This made her even angrier. But, there was nothing she could do. If she ran away they would find her. Then what about the cows that her father already owns?

When evening came and it was time to go to bed this man went to bed early and waited for his wife. When this lady realized what was happening she became more afraid. Well she went to the room and took off her clothes, as she was about to sleep, she changed her mind and decided to run away. She ran out with only a towel around herself. She ran for more than 20 kilometers. She went to her Aunt's house. She wanted to see her aunt's children not her aunt. Her Aunt will definitely send her back. She met the oldest daughter who is studying at the university. She gave her a place to sleep and promised to go with her to the university. They left the next morning. The road to the university passes through the village from which she escaped.

She had to hide because there were people on the road who were looking for her, fortunately, they did not see her. They managed to arrive at the university. She then decided not to go back home, she stayed there for six months. Her parents sent back the cows, but the owner refused them.

Today she is doing her first year at the university and her parents have forgiven her. Praise God.

Early Zulu dwelling for children, elevated to keep animals out.

Mud and grass home in a township outside Lady Smith, South Africa.

Zulu woman cooking lunch.

Squater's camp, poorest of the poor. Just outside Durban, South Africa.

Missions

James Setshogelo

One of the tasks God gave me was to go to Maputo, a city in a foreign country to me [Mozambique]. My mission trip has confirmed my call to missions. Since I knew that God had called me to ministry, I felt only the heart for mission work somewhere in the world. The trip to Maputo has made me realize how much I need to go into the world for God. Maputo mission trip has redirected my life. I saw how much we South Africans have. It is important to thank God for what we have. We have much more on which to survive than the people in Belavista, a settlement near Maputo.

Just a day before I left Maputo, God directed me to see a need in Belavista. Children were working and they were treated poorly. That alone made me seek the face of God. I asked myself, "Why has God made it possible for me to come here?"

For after I asked myself, there came an answer. It is because God has need of my services in Belavista. My life was challenged. While there, I was taken to go and pray for a little child who was very sick. While I was praying I felt God healing that child. That was God confirming my place of service in the field of missions.

I got a vision in Maputo while serving there. That vision is a door for my dream about developing a pre-school for children in Maputo, Belavista. The church to which I belong is in the North West (Jouberton Baptist Church) and has approved my vision and given me permission to go ahead. They even asked the church choir to help me to raise funds for the mission trip. The church choir will be with me for the first ten days in Belavista.

The mission trip to Maputo has awakened a sleeping missionary lion. The call to missionary work was awakened more when I saw the needs of Africans around South Africa. Then when looking at the needs in Maputo, I saw that they can be met by we who are South Africans. Because I've realized that mission is not just about money. It is also about sharing our talents. I have learned some songs from the Belavista brothers and sisters.

The other ingredients are making us available to pray, spreading the good news, and developing a skills training center. People there have a skill of artwork. We can take that and help them to catch fish for themselves. By that I say how can we collect those shells and become partners with them in their craft?

I believe that God has called me to be a missionary. The Maputo mission trip has opened my eyes on this ministry. I have taken a risk by going to Maputo without enough medicine for malaria but no malaria has caught me. That was so powerful for me to witness to my people here in South Africa. Even now I have no malaria sickness. God has protected me from it. For God took good care of me in Maputo, Mozambique.

Mom's Death

James Setshogelo

The year I will never forget: 1997. It was a year in which I gave my life to full-time ministry. Earlier that year I began my college work. I was admitted as a student. My life was being tested. The two first months of the year were very hard. I had no money, my Mother was very sick. She was admitted at the Baragwana Hospital.

She was emotionally troubled. March was a month I was broken to pieces. My Mom was discharged to go home to Mafikena in the North West. It was in March when I received the bad news from my Uncle that she had died. He came to college to tell me. That morning I was in class dealing with Old Testament studies.

My heart started to beat very fast when I saw Jabulani, my Uncle that morning. He came in to ask permission to talk with me. He started mentioning how much he loves me. He mentioned my Mother who loves me. I felt deep in my heart that there is something wrong. He told me that my Mom has left us. By that he meant that my Mom is dead.

My body became so weak that I just collapsed. My uncle carried me to my room. I woke up and tried to return to class and to make sense of all what I heard from him. I could not do it. I broke down in tears in the class. My professor called me outside to ask me what is happening in my life. When I told him, I was not even able to talk about it. He asked me to go to my room and rest. While I was there I could not help it, it was like it is the end of the world to me. I even asked God, "Why have you taken my Mother away from me?" The question was asked in that way because I haven't stayed with my Mother for a long time. She and my Father broke up while I was in grade four. I missed her love and her presence in my life as her child.

The agony I felt made me to be bitter the whole year. Every thing to me was very hard and non-enjoyable. People came to try to give me moral support, but it was painful for a time. The death of my Mother helped me to dig more about "Who am I?" "Why God has called me." I realized that I'm an African man who has to know his culture and traditions.

The death of my mother has made me to be more responsible about the call I received from God. I'm a third child at home. I have remained with a father who re-married another wife. Mom's death brought me loneliness and good memories I will not forget in my whole life. I must follow the same track to help those with a similar experience. I will just say it is not the end of the world when you lose a mother or father. I kept on holding on to Jesus, the source of hope. I kept my faith in God. I prayed about the loss of my mother and met a few people to talk to and tell them how I felt.

I used to rely on crying because it was too hard to cope with such loss. My only question was why my Mom? It was finally answered. How selfish was I to ask that kind of question. God pointed me to a portion of scripture, which says, "The Christ in me is the hope of glory." I asked myself, why do I have to undergo such a painful thing and being so young.

I'm doing my final year in College this year and I have kept by the Christ in me who is the hope of Glory. I wanted to leave or quit the College in 1997 but for God kept me. Jeremiah 29 says, "For I know the plan I have for you." That scripture gave me hope that God loves me and has a plan in my life which I'm to complete somewhere in the world and the church.

In my life I will never forget my mother's good memories and advice she gave me while I was a child and even a month before she died. For her memories will never be forgotten as long as I live. For those who have lost their close loved ones there is Jesus who will never leave them. Day and night he watches over us!! David in Psalm 23 reminds us that the Lord is my shepherd and I shall not want. May we all not want, but fix our hope and eyes unto Jesus the beginner and finisher of our faith.

Loving Your Mom

James Setshogelo

Sitting in my room
Wondering how did things go wrong
To have lost you, death is unfair.
Every night asking myself
What has happened to you Mom.

Hoping daily that you would be there for me
Will I ever see you again Mom? Ever?
Well, the past has gone
But tomorrow is on its way
Help me God to be strong and focused in life
Mom, I need you in my life.
I'm willing to do anything
To be able to see you again.

Loving you
Is the most important memory I have
I don't care what people say
And no one is going to take away my feelings
About you Mom
One thing I can do or say
Is that I love you Mom
Wherever you are
May your soul rest in peace
You will always be loved
Your sons will keep your memories alive.

Participation

William Mokgatle

Lord Jesus I hear you knocking
At the door of my heart
As a South African man
Who is glued to his ancestral beliefs
Prove to me that you are God.

Lord Jesus you know my African culture.
You have become a part of my native ways.
You have participated with me in my affairs.
You fully understand me.

You have walked with me and dine with me.
You have corrected my wrongs, my indifferences and
my values.
You know that I am Culture-bound.
You have helped me in my choices.

You never got tired of my presence.
For you wanted me to be a new creature.
You are God and ruler of all cultures.
Cultureless you are with my ethics and values.
Your participation in my life
Fits well with all my strengths and weaknesses.

You are the creator of the universe.
You are the designer of all creatures.

You have spoken and worlds have come to be.
Thus all creatures great and small have been touched
by you.
You clearly know everyone of them.
None escape your memories or are outside your awareness.

God's Hands

William Mokgatle

Lord, help me to realize that
My tomorrows are in your hands.
They are under your control.
My tomorrows belong to you.

Lord, help me to realize that
Even my yesterday was in your hand.
It too was under your control.
My yesterdays were yours.

Lord, help me to realize that
My today is in your hands.
It is under your control.
My today is yours.

Lord, help me realize that
You do not make mistakes with your hand.
I am under your control.
I belong to you.

Looking back I realize that
Lord you have loved me with your warm hands.
You have guided me with your hands.
I am happy you did.

Sweet Jesus I realize that
I was not worth keeping in your hands.
Abundantly you gave to me while under your control.
I cannot measure it all.

I realize that
My friend's hands are different from your hands
They do not control with love.
Their motives are so different from yours.

Son of God, I realize that
I am privileged to be in your hands.
Being under your control
Is far better than anything in this world.

If only I could remember that
The price you paid for me was in God's hands.
You died a sinner's death for me.
I must now look within.

It is my duty to realize that
I must never try to escape from your hands
It's worth staying under your control
No matter what I may reason.

Reality is realizing that
If I die today in your hands
Spreading the gospel in your hands
Will prove to the world
That truly I am yours.

This gives me courage that
I should live as though I am in your hands.
So that your message of your hands
Will be heard by those who need to be touched by
your hands.

Zulu Warriors

David Moloi

It was just after sunset when I heard some men talking outside. My father, three sisters, two brothers and I were at home. I opened the back door just when my elder brother, who had arrived from a drinking spree, opened the door to the toilet to come out. Two strangers were waiting for him to come out. One of the strangers hit my brother with a slap. He retaliated. The second man was standing ready with a huge stone in his hand. Without thinking, I found myself in the air, going for the second man who was ready to hit my brother with a stone. I managed to push him off balance so he could not hit my brother with the stone. To be honest, even today, I don't understand how I got myself in the air, jumping onto the stranger with a stone. I do not know what gave those guys such a fright that they ran for their dear lives out of our yard. We only realized after they ran away that they were Zulus.

My brother knew that they would be coming back and he just disappeared. They did come back an hour later with many more Zulu warriors carrying all sorts of weapons. Their knock on the front door of our home suggested that they were in the spirit of war. Many people know that when the Zulu warriors attack, they create havoc wherever they go.

I answered the knock, and prayed the shortest prayer I had ever prayed, "Lord help me." The Zulu warriors flocked into the house and demanded my brother who they thought

was the one who tried to rob them before they followed him to my home. There were so many that I could not have counted them. Many more were waiting outside. They were fuming with anger. Psalm 91 ran through my mind, as well as Psalm 23, "even though I walk through the valley of the shadow of death, I will fear no evil." The Word of God was real and I was not afraid of this evil. God took over in my life and I got calm. I explained to them that my brother was not in and that he did not try to rob them as he was too drunk to have tried that.

My two sisters hid under the bed. My father joined us from his bedroom and tried to talk to them. They would not listen to him. In fact they were on the verge of hitting my father as well. When I spoke to them, they would listen. Then one of my sisters tried to reason with them. They promised to hit her, so she had to keep quiet. I was just amazed to find that the only person they would listen to was me. I give God the glory because of His enveloping power that rendered the angry Zulu warriors powerless and unable to hurt us. They left without causing any damage whatsoever. That was unlike the Zulu warriors on the attack. God is great; "no weapon that is formed against thee shall prosper," Isaiah 54:17. God hears and answers prayer. Even the shortest prayer, He is able to respond to it. May God have the glory.

Staring

William Mokgatle

Staring at you today with
With disbelief and shame
Leaves me speechless that you
Intended to love me without conditions.

Staring at you today
With disbelief and shame
Encourages me to feel good about myself.
You truly meant to change me.
You intended to change me for the best.

Staring at you today
With conscious mind and without shame
Strengthens me to tell the word,
That you humbled yourself to bring about change.
You intended that your love extend to all of us.

Staring at you today
I am perplexed and overjoyed.
My Spirit is lifted high and singing.
I am praising and testifying to all people.
You have shown us your ways.

Touching and hugging you today
With pride and happiness
Fulfills in me your greatness.
You are highest to us all.
You truly deserve to be praised.

Stewardship

David Moloi

It was in the early seventies when I came to know Jesus as my personal Savior. Soon thereafter I was preaching the Gospel in the trains and buses. I felt God's calling into full time ministry in the late eighties, but was distracted by the fact that God was using me to reach out to thousands of people. I thought to myself that there was no need to go full time. The urge to go to a theological college grew stronger as the years went by. I shared this with my wife who gave me a blank refusal. Her negative reply was prompted by the fact that she was a Baptist Pastor's daughter. The family went through difficult times during and after her father's stay at the Bible College. Well, I made a decision never to go into full time ministry unless my wife agreed to it.

Then I prayed to God and presented four requests to him. Which, if He would supply one after another, would give us a sure indication that it was God who was calling me into full time ministry. First, my wife should be willing to let me go to college. Second, that God would supply me with finances for the college, and that my family shall have no financial needs. Third, that God would provide us with a house. Fourth, that God would bless us as a family with healthy bodies.

A friend of ours invited us to visit them in England in 1996, and paid airfares for my wife and I to go. One man, out of all the people we had met, was interested my call to min-

istry. He wanted to know what I was doing as well as what I intended doing. I shared with him about my talk with the Lord and the requests that I put before him. It ended there, and he never said a word to me.

Toward the end of 1996, I received a phone call from Britain. Our friend there promised to pay for my school fees for the three years that I will be at the college. By then the Lord had already provided us with a house in Orlando [a neighborhood in Soweto, the large township outside Johannesburg] just as I requested Him. My joy knew no bounds when my wife gave me an okay to go and study at the college, which is Baptist Convention College. I can tell you that our friend in Britain has kept his promise to this day. He is continuing to give his money to enable me to pursue my theological studies. It is sowing time for him. In due course he will be reaping just as it is written in Galatians 6:7 ". . . A man reaps what he sows."

As a result of our friend's stewardship in money, I believe that we are now partners with him. He has a share in whichever way the Lord uses me in this ministry. I Samuel 30:24 "The share of the man who stayed with the supplies is to be the same as that of him who went down to the battle. All will share alike."

Our friend will have a share in all the people I will lead to the Lord, though he will be thousands of kilometers away from South Africa. Why? His stewardship allowed me to be trained as a pastor. Our friend will be there with me that day when the saints are rewarded. We will share with him. That is stewardship at its best.

Equipped to Be Busy

Pumelelo

I spent my holidays in God's work. When I arrived at home from school, there was a brother who was waiting for me. He was asked by the church leadership to assist me. We were starting cell group meetings, helping the church choir and organizing a Gospel concert. The brother is Luyanda. He works for Youth for Christ as a missionary in evangelism. He is talented in music, trained to start cell groups and leadership trainings and gifted in teaching. I was privileged to work with such a man.

We started with cell group meeting in five stations. All are at a far distance from one another and where we stay. We were often traveling by foot and at other times by public transport. We used our money to go to all these stations. In all of them we were taking an hour for introducing and informing about the purposes and importance of a cell group meeting. We were arriving earlier than other members while they were late and our time was too long in each station. This has caused me to not have enough time with other friends and relatives at home. The time we were taking in the stations is more than two and a half hours.

On Tuesdays and Thursdays we were with the choir for practices. We were preparing for the Gospel concert and a wedding. The choir was to perform in both functions. In a choir practice we were spending five hours. We were helping them to train their voices, to listen to the music instruments, to dance with songs and to learn new songs.

We also had the leadership training for those who will be leading the cell groups. We took the entire afternoon on Saturday. After that I was leading the cell groups to show the new leaders how to facilitate. I was organizing a concert. On some Sundays I was preaching, then I was preparing messages or sermons.

Lastly I went with some young people to a summer camp. I was responsible for that trip. After camp I organized a youth get together in this new year. I prepared a program and became the director for that meeting.

In all, I spent my time, finance, gifts and skill in working for the Lord in the church. This has only been possible because God has supplied all my needs according to his riches in glory. This is what God has called and prepared me to do.

Do unto Others

Thuli Manola

In January 1997, I went to Johannesburg looking for a school for my little boy. We had no money to carry us through the whole year. I did not even know how the school fees of my son would be paid. After an interview by the director of the school, she offered me a job as an assistant teacher. It was afterwards that she found out that I was not working but was a theological student. I was able to pay my son's school fees and have a plate of food on our table.

I was not getting much money. I thought of some other students in the convention college who needed financial support. Inside me something told me to take my tithe and share it among them. Every month the men students would get some cash. I brought the women students cosmetics. I was challenged by the young boy in Matthew 14:19. I learned that no matter how small a thing is, it is the motive that counts the most. These students had no source of income while preparing themselves to be pastors. Water alone was not sufficient for taking care of their bodies. They needed soap to smell like normal people. I had to share with them, knowing that at the other side I was expected to provide at home since I was the only one working.

No one asked to be adopted by me. Something inside me kept revealing their need. I felt that I needed to take the responsibility for helping them. It did not become much of a burden for me to do that.

I was challenged by something that happened to me the year before I was employed. Recall that there was no one working at home. There was a Pastor who delivered food parcels in our community every week. He came to our home and saw how hard we were pulling. God touched him and he became a good steward by sharing his resources with us.

Since I was working it gave me the opportunity to help others where it was needed. I did not say that my income is mine and for my family. Nor did I say that I could not share with strangers. Deep in my mind it was a right thing to do. I had no doubt for a moment. I think it is very important that we listen to that voice that speaks to us through others. Things happen for a reason. I personally knew how needy these brethren were. Earning money did not cause me to forget them. They were always there in my thoughts. Sharing with them made me see myself as a true ambassador of God. They say experience is a best teacher, what was offered to me in time of need made me see the need of sharing when I was trusted by God with resources of my own.

All of Life

Dorah Maotoe

Stewardship simply means the care and responsible use of God's gifts. For us to be good stewards, we need to be good managers of what God has given into our care. Human beings are expected by God to be good stewards of one's body, time, money, environment, relationships, God's word, discipleship, talents, etc. All of the above factors are free gifts from God.

In my church, we are still struggling to catch up with giving and tithing, but there is a special family that challenged and still challenges me when coming to giving. We once had a problem of how to pay one of our brothers who cleans the church every Saturday. This family pledged to pay the money every month indefinitely without grumbling. They are also supporting a certain widow in our church. They do it monthly and they do this cheerfully. What challenges us mostly as a church is that we see God blessing them day after day, and the more they give, the more they receive. This has taught me that we need to take God at his word.

I also want to thank God that he gave me an opportunity to express my gratitude to him by being a good steward of his young ones. I am a Sunday school teacher but I am doing more than that. I often gather children, even those who are not saved, on a particular Saturday and teach them God's word, games, choruses and other traditional dances that will finally bring them to loving God. I spend so much time with kids and learn from them how much they love the Lord and identify their needs. I am always ready to be with these kids who are so neglected and marginalized.

As a member of the "Social Ministry Committee" in my church, I find it challenging to serve God together with someone who does not have anything to do after the service. I made it my responsibility to identify such people, even those who have no schooling because of lack of money. These people are cared for in my church and a bursary scheme is in operation to cater to such a need. As a Committee we visit the elders, those in hospitals, those who cannot attend due to illness or insufficient funds for transport.

In my region we thank God for our local women's department. They organize rallies and workshops whereby women are taught, especially those who are in the leadership. In the two workshops I have attended, we were taught about stewardship. I was so challenged that I began to pray about it. As a vice secretary in 1996, I brought about great changes in our church executive. God gave me a gift of discernment. I want things in order and things to be done here and now. So I introduced the organization of records, which for years has not been done in our church. All details pertaining to membership, correspondence and any other records were there (letterheads, interview forms, hymnals, thank you cards for visitors, church stamp, etc). I saw to it that they are all in place. God taught me that we have to be more like professionals in order to lead exemplary lives to our followers. We need to take care of all the resources as a leadership. Those we do to glorify God and Him alone. Our Pastor is also a good steward of time. Everybody knows that he will always come first every Sunday and everything should be done within the stipulated time, to make use of every opportunity we have. God expects us to be good stewards of the time he has entrusted to us.

Cancer

Freda Moidil

My name is Freda and I'm 24 years old. I'm a born-again Christian and I love the Lord with all my heart. In June 1998 I had some lumps removed on my breast and as I was only 23 years old there was no fear that it could be anything serious. In 1999 I had another lump growing everyday on my right breast and I was very worried. I went to the hospital to remove the lump on the 16th February 1999.

On the 22nd February I went to get the results and I was so confident because I just knew that it was just a growth like the first one. The doctor told me that they found cancer on my breast. I could not believe it and I was just waiting for the doctor to say that he was only joking. But no one can joke with something so serious. I felt that the doctor was very cruel to tell me that. I just cried. He then told me that he is going to remove my breast. I just could not imagine losing my breast. That is when I realized how important is each and every part of our bodies. We have to cherish it and always thank God for our body. It was very difficult and that was the most terrible day of my life. I had to choose as to whether I keep my breast and let the cancer spread or lose my breast and stop the cancer from spreading.

I had to make a decision very fast because they wanted to do the surgery a day after I heard the news. I asked for a day and I talked to my fellow Christians and they gave me all the support that I needed. I prayed for strength and I knew that the Lord would be with me through everything. I meditated on Psalm 23 and I knew that "even though I walk through the valley of the shadow of death, I will fear no evil."

I had a mastectomy to remove of one of my breasts on the 25th February 1999. Even though it was so difficult I thank God because he gave me the strength, strong faith and the positive mind. I believe that everything is going to turn out just fine. I have been in pain for a long time and also living with the idea of coping with my loss. I had counseling and also a lot of support from my church and friends. I started the cancer treatment, Chemotherapy and Radiotherapy in March 1999. My first chemo treatment was terrible, I was very sick. I still cry when I think about that day. I thank God because I did not give up but I kept my faith and continued with my treatment.

I was supposed to have eight treatments of chemo but unfortunately they had to add four more treatments. The excitement of finishing the treatment was gone and I just cried. I was very disappointed. Still I took heart and continued with the treatment. I'm left with two treatments which I'm going to finish in March 00. I just pray that this is now going to be the last time. I know that God cares, He knows what I'm going through and he is working everything out for me. I still feel sick after the chemotherapy. But, I have told myself that this will pass.

I thank God for the job that He blessed me with, because I have a good medical aid that enables me to get a good treatment. My life is so different ever since I was diagnosed with the disease. I'm closer to God. I'm positive with everything I do and willing to face any challenge that may come my way.

Editor's note: Freda died two months later, overtaken by cancer. She was still praising God for walking with her through this dark journey.

Tough Times

Thandeka

Nobody told me that when I became saved things would go smooth. No one told me that I wouldn't have problems or suffer. But believe me, I have always convinced myself that life would be better, circumstances would improve, and people would change. I was wrong. My heart was severely broken. I was disappointed. I was cast down. I was depressed.

It was my first month at the Training Academy when my mother lost her job. Although she was not earning much as a housekeeper, she was able to pay my monthly school fees. I started to realize how easy it is to trust God when you have some source of help. To me this was the hardest test. My source was taken away. I knew that God is a provider but in my situation I was tempted to doubt that. I saw my faith wavering. My hope was dying.

I continued attending classes. I know what it means to trust God out of nothing. There was a time I felt like giving up. Everything was not going well. Every morning I woke up with a heavy head and heart, because I knew that I would be reminded to pay my fees. At the end of the fourth month, I received a statement. If I don't pay within 7 days I won't be allowed to attend classes. That's what it was saying. I didn't show it to my mom. I was hurting. My soul was cracking.

On that weekend I visited a missionary couple. I came to know them through a friend, Luvuyo. I enjoyed their company very much. They were so good to me, so loving and caring. I didn't say anything about the statement I received. The following day we went to church. After the church service, the missionary wife came to me. She was holding something in her hand. She gave it to me. It was money, R200. I couldn't believe it. While I was still standing shaking with disbelief she came again. "Papa Dan also wanted you to have this. We understand your situation and if you need anything else just let us know." She said all of that with eyes full of love. I didn't know what to say. My words were not enough to express my thankfulness. The only thing I managed to say is a soft "Thank you." I couldn't believe it. It was like someone will come and tell me I was dreaming.

The following day I couldn't wait to go to school. I was filled with joy. I paid my fees, and although I didn't pay all the debt, the money I paid was enough to stabilize my account. I continued trusting in the Lord and Papa Dan and Mama Sandy continued with their support, financially and spiritually. I believe it was their daily prayer that God might open their eyes to the needs of people. They didn't only see my needs, they met them.

Believe me, the road was not easy for me. There are nights I cried myself to sleep. Nothing was beautiful in my eyes. I hated life. But in all those situations I held on to my faith, I held on to Jesus. I knew that better days would come. I was strengthened by the Lord's presence in me. I was not alone although sometimes I felt forsaken.

Jesus was able to carry me through. At the end of the year I received my Diploma in Business Administration. The day I went to fetch it, believe me when I say I was no longer a young girl crying for mom, I was a woman who went to a battle and came back victorious. I was a woman who knows what it means to be carried by the Lord, for I remember very well the days I lay in the ditch like a broken bird, unable to fly and God kept on strengthening me. He kept on assuring me of His love and He kept on reminding me that those who wait upon Him will not only renew their strength, they will soar on wings like eagles. He was there with me. I was not alone.

Today I am working and I thank God for the missionaries who helped me find this job. I spent many months unable to

get a job. They are always intervening at the lowest and saddest times of my life. In my heart I am convinced that God is taking me somewhere and what I'm doing here is just the beginning of God's plan and purposes. THE BEST IS YET TO COME.

Take Me

Sipho Khanyile

Oh Father won't you just take me to the place I long for
The place where I will never want or need
Take me to the land where your will rules over all
Take me to that world where your ordinances are food of life
How long shall we see abominable acts and abuse of the
small and old
Abba Father please take me to Your safety before I go astray.

I have enjoyed living on this earth
But now I feel lonely and morose
My soul is overworked by sorrows and distressed
Take me to the land where God governs over all
My heart is longing for that godly place
Take me to the land of peace and tranquility
I mean the land where there is no jealousy
Please take me to that land of harmony

Take me to the land where wealth is not an issue
To a world where there is no hunger and agony
The land full of happiness and everlasting eternity
Where there is no beggar, rich or poor take me there
To the place where I will own nothing except life eternal
Lead me to the land where tears are not shed

My soul is in struggle every day and night
Trying to address the problems and challenges faced
Many a time I have no solutions and remedies
My prayer is always a question of how long!
Jesus! How long?
It is far from me to resort to any other means of solution
Father would you be kind enough to transfer to me
another place

Then God the Almighty responded to my plea
My child the land you are crying for is the very place where
you live
It is not the world that needs to change it is you
All you need for today is found in my only begotten Son
All you need is the right key to your future
To miss the key is to miss your future. Jesus is the only Key.

God Who Cares

Sipho Khanyile

I know that the Lord cares for me
He has taught me a lot along this way
He gave me courage, wisdom and strength
I must walk along his way.

I know that the Lord gave me life
He died for me on the cross
He saved me from death when I was lost
I now must walk his way.

I know that Jesus healed me
His stripes and His death of shame
He proved to the world that truly I'm His
I am called to love in his name.

I know that Jesus watches over me
He saved me from death many times
He always sent His angels during my dire need
There are daily provisions that are mine.

I know Jesus you are perfect
You are loving, faithful and good
You care even for those who don't
For you are God of the brotherhood.

The Other Side

Sipho Khanyile

The other side,
Just what is the other side?
Why must there be another side?
Why do people depend so much on the other side?
Why is the other side so important?

When I state my case confidently and bravely,
There is you, the other side.
You are considered the greatest
And my case is measured by you, the other side.

Other side, "who are you?"
Who are you to be considered?
To whom are you accountable?
Why are you so influential?
Why do people make you, the other side, a reference for me?

After all has been said and done,
Then comes you! The other side
People start doubting "my side"
My side loses its substance and appeal
To you, the other side.

No one supports me
Without looking at you the other side
After I have stated my case with great hope for acceptance;
You, the other side,
Have weakened my case and left me to be small.

Where should I complain about you, the other side?
To whom must I report you, the other side?
When will I enjoy your sympathy and compassion,
other side?
When will your ideas coincide with my side?

Come on, other side. Talk!
Can we even agree to disagree?
Let us reconcile to one another.
Let the hatred that exists between us
Come to an end.
Let us do away with our indifference toward each other.

Finally the other side responds.
"As much as I would like to comply, I cannot."
So the other side remains the other side.
The differences, the conflict, the pain
Are born of the prince of the *Other Side*.

Thanksgiving

David Moloi

One morning the Holy Spirit spoke to me about praising God and giving Him thanks in times when I didn't really want to. It all started when I lost my credit cards, in fact all my credit cards in a credit card holder. It was in the afternoon, when I had just knocked off, somewhere in Bree Street on my way to a bus stop. I realized that my cards were missing. I felt so bad that I was miserable. I kept asking myself why it must be me? No answer. When I got home I told my wife who joined me in that state of misery. We prayed together, asking God to undertake for us in that situation.

When I woke up the following day, I was still feeling bad inside. My prayer to God seemed to be very empty. I was sitting in a bus on my way to work when the Holy Spirit spoke to me right in that hour of frustration and confusion. He said to me "Why don't you try thanking and praising God?" I objected there and then, even without thinking. I said, "How can I praise and thank God when I have lost all my cards?" Somehow I was getting more and more irritated because I did not have an answer why He allowed those credit cards to get lost.

It was after a space of about fifteen minutes when the same voice that spoke to me earlier repeated the same question: "Why don't you try thanking and praising God?" I immediately realized that God was talking to me and I obeyed. You will understand that I had never prayed such a prayer to God before. It was difficult. My mind did not want me to pray like that because it did not make any sense. It was like my entire body was giving out a negative response against what God said for me to do.

I can remember clearly, covering my mouth with a palm of one hand to thank and praise Him that I had lost my credit cards. The more I thanked and praised Him, the more it became difficult to say those words of thanksgiving and praise. But somehow I felt the peace of God welling up in the inside of me, and I was greatly encouraged to praise Him more and more. I even told God that I did not understand why I was thanking and praising Him the way I did. All the same I did offer Him praise and thanksgiving.

Just when I had finished locking up the company's offices, an unknown man walked out of one of the two lifts, greeted me and inquired if I was David Moloi. Impulsively, I jumped and responded with a question, "Did you find them?" The man said, "Yes, and they are here intact." He gave me the credit cards and not one was missing. That man can tell you better about the things I did and said in joy and excitement. I reached for my pen and paper so that I could write down his particulars, but he refused to give them to me. I tried to beg him to give me his name, and he still refused. The lift's doors opened and off he went. To this day I do not know who that man is. All times I am tempted to believe that that was not just a man. This was an angel of God.

From that day I learned a lesson about the power of thanksgiving and praise. "In everything give thanks" has a new meaning in my life as a Christian. Many Christians have been blessed by this testimony. It has helped them to release the power of thanksgiving and praise in every situation, good or bad. To God be the glory.

Words of Wisdom

Sipho Khanyile

Be kind to people who are desperate
Offer means and ways to solve problems.
Never promise anything to the needy
But involve the needy in finding help for themselves.
It is better to practice support than preach support.
Never treat symptoms of a problem but rather treat the
cause.

Never become too excited about your own success
Rather engage yourself in the next thing to do.
Be careful of people who lift you up because of your success
They are the ones who will drop you down.
Don't be used by people but help people.
Never demand respect but respect every person.

Wise use of money can be the source of much joy in life
But the love of money is a cancer of the mind.
Abstain from focusing on positions and titles
Rather focus on the needs of the community.
As a leader, represent the community you lead
Rather than representing your own interests.

Abstain from speaking lies.
Let faithful be your everyday language.
Never be naïve about the inclinations and needs
Of people who have confidence in you.
Never appear to be wise
But impart the wisdom in you to the people you lead.

Always seek to find wisdom for people when they appear to
be unwise
Never underestimate other people's interest.
Beware not to judge people according to what
they appear to be.
But rather see them for who they really are.
Love people who criticize you
More than those who shake your hand and pat
your shoulder.

South African Stories

True Stories of Faith, Hardship and Deliverance from
the Hearts and Pens of Black South Africans

ISBN 0-9720620-1-7

This book is available direct from the publisher, or can be
ordered through your favorite bookstore.

To order direct from the publisher send $13.95 for each copy.
Add $4.00 shipping and handling for the first copy, plus
another $1.00 for each additional copy. Maximum shipping
costs $25.00. Maine residents add 5% sales tax.

Please send ____copies to:

Name: _____

Address: _____

_____

Phone number (optional) _____

e-mail address (optional) _____

(Phone numbers and e-mail addresses will be used for customer service only.
Information will remain private.)

Total amount enclosed:_____

Please send check or money order to North Wind Publishing,
P.O. Box 192, Rockport, ME 04856.

Quantity discounts: 10–25 copies, $12.00 each;
over 25 copies; $11.00 each.

Bookstores: Distributed by FaithWorks, a division
of the National Book Network; 1-877-323-4550
(www.faithworksonline.com).